Remote Work Revolution
Tips for Thriving in a New Era

Table of Contents

Chapter 1. Introduction

Welcome to a brave new world, the frontier of the Remote Work Revolution! Our Special Report takes you on a journey of adapting, thriving, and excelling in this digitally-connected, home-office era. Brace yourself for real-life stories, expert insights, and an arsenal of handy tips and tricks aimed at facilitating your transition into remote work. Not only will this guide be your lighthouse in successfully navigating the challenges of the virtual workspace, it's also designed to foster a vibrant sense of community, even when situated miles apart from your colleagues. Your professional life is about to gain a fresh perspective and a breath of new energy. All this, and more, is but a purchase away, in our Special Report. Step into the future with confidence and poise, ready to conquer the world right from your living room!

Chapter 2. The Dawn of the Remote Work Era

In a matter of months, the world, as we knew it, changed dramatically due to the Covid-19 pandemic. As public health measures escalated, working in physical office spaces became a luxury few could afford. Millions, almost overnight, found themselves in a situation they hadn't foreseen or planned for - working from home.

2.1. Work from Home - The Unexpected Beginning

Who could've predicted that so many people around the globe would suddenly be thrust into remote working? Pre-pandemic work models, based on nine-to-five schedules based in physical spaces, evaporated overnight. Companies had to pivot quickly to ensure their teams could efficiently work from home while managing the inevitable teething problems, such as connectivity issues, lack of appropriate hardware, and even adapting to new methods of communication and scheduling.

Despite the challenges, people found ways to manage, mainly because they had no other option. Many, however, discovered unexpected benefits from this new working model – reduced commuting time, a more flexible schedule, a better work-life balance.

2.2. The Evidence: Remote Work, Here to Stay

Fast forward a year, and a clear trend emerged. Many employees were not eager to go back to the office full time. Though they missed certain aspects of office life, such as personal interactions with colleagues, they found that the advantages outweighed these elements.

Microsoft's Work Trend Index 2020 discovered that 82% of managers expected to have more flexible work-from-home policies post-pandemic, and 71% of employees wanted to continue to work from home at least part time. Another study from Buffer indicated that over 90% of workers wouldn't go back to office life as it was before.

So, the dawn of the remote work era didn't just arise out of necessity, it thrived because many employees and employers alike found it be a significantly efficient and effective mode of work.

2.3. Mapping the Benefits

Work from home has clear benefits on many levels. For employees, it often means a better work-life balance, the end of long commuting hours, and the ability to create a more personalized work environment.

For employers, it can lead to reduced costs, greater access to a diverse talent pool, and measurable increases in productivity. A 2020 report by Prodoscore, based on data from 30,000 workers, showed a 47% increase in worker productivity compared to the prior year.

Environmental impacts should not be underestimated either. Think of the gallons of petrol not burned, the tons of carbon dioxide not emitted due to the drastic reduction in commuting!

2.4. Fostering New Habits: Key to Successful Remote Work

Acquiring the right set of skills and habits is crucial in successfully adapting to remote work. This requires both individuals and organizations to be in sync and cultivate a positive remote work culture.

Key to this is communication. With the right tools - think video conferencing apps, chat applications, and project management tools - remote work doesn't have to be isolating. Daily check-ins and updates can keep the team connected and informed. It's important to remember that it's not only about work-related communication; chatting about hobbies or sharing a virtual lunch is also key to maintaining morale and fostering a sense of connectedness.

Self-discipline becomes even more crucial when working from home. With distractions aplenty and no boss looking over your shoulder, individuals need to cultivate good habits through structured work schedules and to-do lists, ensuring productivity doesn't falter.

2.5. The Challenges

Of course, the dawn of the remote work era is not without its challenges. The physical separation from colleagues can cause a sense of isolation. Balancing work and personal life may be difficult, especially when your work and living space blend into one.

Another hurdle is the decrease in spontaneous idea generation that comes from in-person interactions. It's important for organizations to tackle these issues head-on, as ignoring them may lead to burnout, decreased morale, and ultimately, lower productivity.

Despite these hurdles, the numerous advantages of remote work make it a promising prospect. As we progress into its era, we must remember that just as with any change, patience, resilience, and adaptability will play crucial roles in determining the longevity and success of this new work construct.

Chapter 3. Becoming a Remote Work Success: Traits and Skills

Switching to a remote work environment may seem like a daunting task, but with the right tools and mindset, you can thrive in this new frontier. To succeed in being a remote employee, it's critical to cultivate certain traits and skills. These do not just make you productive but allow you to seamlessly integrate work and personal life, create enduring professional relationships, and extract the maximum benefit from virtual collaboration. This transition will involve refining your existing repertoire and honing new traits and strategies.

3.1. Developing Self-Discipline and Time Management Skills

Remote work demands a high level of self-discipline and excellent time management abilities. Without the external structure of a traditional workplace, it's up to you to prioritize tasks, set deadlines, manage distractions, and maintain a balanced work-life equilibrium.

1. Set daily and weekly goals. Break down larger projects into manageable tasks and deadlines over the course of the week.

2. Avoid distractions. Designate a workspace and establish household protocols to limit interruptions during work hours.

3. Take regular breaks. Remote work often blurs work-life boundaries, leading to longer hours. Incorporate breaks to stay fresh and guard against burnout.

3.2. Building Efficient Communication Skills

Without face-to-face encounters, communication can be challenging in a remote work setting. Acquiring excellent written and verbal communication skills becomes imperative.

1. Be clear and concise. Avoid ambiguity and be direct in your communication.

2. Regular updates. Keep your team informed about your progress regularly.

3. Use appropriate tools. Different modes of communication (email, chat, video calls) are suitable for different circumstances. Choose wisely.

3.3. Acquiring Technical Skills

Technology is the backbone of remote work. Familiarize yourself with digital tools that facilitate virtual team collaboration, project management, and communication. Stay informed about cyber safety practices to protect sensitive data.

1. Use appropriate software. Know your team's preferred tools, and get comfortable using them.

2. Ensure data safety. Use secure networks and strong security software.

3. Back-up your work. Keep your data in more than one location in case of a technological glitch.

3.4. Nurturing Emotional Intelligence

An often overlooked but an important aspect of remote work success is emotional intelligence (EI). The ability to perceive, manage, and express one's emotions effectively, while also understanding and responding to the emotions of others, can foster better collaboration within remote teams.

1. Be empathetic. Understand the constraints and pressures your colleagues might be under.

2. Facilitate open dialogue. Encourage team discussions about challenges and solutions in a remote work context.

3. Stay positive. Maintain a positive attitude to foster a healthier work environment.

3.5. Strengthening Self-Motivation

The lack of immediate oversight in remote work scenarios makes self-motivation an invaluable trait. It can guide you through difficult tasks, spur creativity, and keep you performing at high levels even when you're physically alone.

1. Set personal goals. Strive to exceed your own expectations.

2. Seek professional growth. Treat remote work as an opportunity not just to perform a role, but also to expand your skillset.

3. Celebrate achievements. Recognize and reward yourself for hitting milestones and targets. Remember, your motivation fuels your productivity.

3.6. Understanding Remote Work Etiquettes

Just because the communication in a remote work setup is virtual, it doesn't mean manners and etiquette take a backseat. Learning and adhering to best practices in virtual communication will help maintain professionalism and show respect for your colleagues' time.

1. Be punctual for virtual meetings. This shows respect for the other participants' time.

2. Dress appropriately for video calls. This signals commitment and a professional mindset.

3. Respond swiftly. Acknowledge receipt of communication and aim to respond within a reasonable timescale, so others aren't left in uncertainty.

Embracing remote work is a continuous learning journey. Cultivating the right traits and honing the necessary skills require time, patience, and practice. Remember, this transition is not just about surviving but thriving and making the most of the opportunities that remote work offers. Keep exploring, keep learning, and, above all, remember that the key to becoming a remote work success lies in adaptability and resilience. You're not merely surviving the Remote Work Revolution; you're leading it!

Chapter 4. Setting the Stage: Your Ideal Home Office

The right environment is a key to nurturing any successful endeavor, and setting up your home office is no exception. Crafting the physical space around which your professional life revolves requires careful thought and planning. This chapter will guide you in designing a home office that aligns your workspace with your working style, ensuring productivity and focus while maintaining balance with your personal life.

4.1. The Blueprint: Plan Ahead

Before rushing to purchase your first office chair or desk, it's critical to envision the layout of your home workspace. The size, floor layout, natural light availability, and noise situations must be considered. After all, your home office should serve to replicate, if not enhance, the traditional office environment suitable to your work style.

Ask yourself questions like: - Will you be conducting a lot of video calls requiring a good background and professional lighting? - Do you thrive in an abundant natural light setting or does a cosy, warmly-lit corner sound more inviting? - How much physical space can you dedicate to your home office without encroaching on your personal life?

Only after careful consideration of these factors should you move on to purchasing your furniture and equipment. It's not merely about filling a room with furniture, but improving productivity without compromising comfort.

4.2. Spare no Expense: Office Furniture

While it may be tempting to economize on office furniture, remember that this is an investment in your health, productivity, and professional longevioty. Your chair and desk form the physical foundation of your workday, getting these aspects right is paramount.

Ergonomic chair: Protect your back and posture with an ergonomically designed chair. Adjustable height, armrests, and back support are features to look for, ensuring comfort across long hours of work.

Adjustable desk: Consider investing in a height-adjustable desk that can be used both sitting and standing. This provides flexibility and prevents the health problems associated with excessive sitting.

Office lighting: Workplaces need proper lighting to reduce eye-strain and maintain alertness. Utilize a mixture of natural and artificial lighting to create a pleasant, efficient work environment.

4.3. Technology Check: Essential Gadgets

As you step into the digital world of remote work, equip your home office with the requisite technologies. This includes a reliable computer, high-speed internet connection, and necessary software applications.

Computer: Whether it's a desktop or a laptop, ensure your machine can handle your work requirements.

Internet: Prioritize fast and reliable internet connections. No one wants to be stuck with buffering video calls or painfully slow downloads!

Software: From email clients to project management and collaborative tools, have your software applications installed and ready.

Readily available IT support: Set up access to remote IT support to address unexpected technical glitches.

4.4. Ambience: Create a Productive Environment

Design an environment that primes your brain for productivity. This may include:

Cleanliness: Keep your workspace tidy and clutter-free.

Noise Control: Use noise-cancelling headphones or white noise machines to drown out disturbing noises.

Personalization: Consider adding plants, pictures, motivational quotes, or any other personal items that inspire you.

In your home office, recreate the benefits of a traditional office while also taking advantage of the fact that you can personalize it to optimize your productivity and comfort.

4.5. Boundaries: Keep Work and Personal Life Separate

Ensure that you have a clearly defined physical boundary between your work and personal spaces. Close the door when you're working, if you can. Use rugs or room dividers if needed. This will help set psychological boundaries and enable you to switch off from work more easily.

Remember, setting up your home office is a process, and it's okay to continually tweak it as you discover what works best for you. So, pore over these tips, but feel free to adjust and personalize. The beauty of your home office lies in the freedom it offers to design a space that works uniquely for you. Your office should not only provide functional support for executing tasks but also contribute to overall well-being and job satisfaction. Be patient with yourself and allow some time for adjustment and fine-tuning – and most importantly, make sure to enjoy the process!

Chapter 5. Time Management and Productivity in the Digital World

In the era of remote work, time management and productivity have become crucial elements that shape our professional success. While the convenience of a home office is appealing, it also brings unique challenges. Let's delve into the strategies we can adopt to harness our hours and ramp up productivity in our digital terrain.

5.1. Embracing a Structured Day

Start your remote work journey by recreating the structure of a normal office day at home. This means having a regular start and end time daily, scheduled breaks, and setting aside specific slots for tasks to maintain rhythm and routine. As studies show, humans thrive on routines, which create a sense of order and control, fostering productivity.

```
Morning: It's your start line. Structure it to gain
momentum throughout the day. Whether it's meditating,
working out, or reading, indulge in an activity that
fuels you for the day ahead.
Work-hours: Delineate your working hours. Avoid chores
or personal tasks during this time. Display commitment,
as if you are in an actual office environment.
Breaks: Timely and deliberate breaks prevent burnout.
Step away from your workspace and do something non-work
related to rejuvenate your mind.
After-hours: Protect your personal time post-work.
Engage in relaxation or hobbies to maintain a healthy
```

5.2. Setting Clear Goals and Priorities

The sheer number of tasks at hand might seem overwhelming at times. To combat this, prioritize and set clear, achievable goals. Use frameworks like Eisenhower's Decision Matrix or the ABCDE method:

5.3. Becoming Tech-Savvy

Leveraging technology is instrumental in increasing productivity. Use tools like time trackers, digital calendars, project management software, or even smart AI assistants. These can help streamline your workflow, reduce manual labor, and keep distractions at bay.

5.4. Creating a Conducive Work Environment

An organized and conducive workspace proves to be less distracting and more inspiring. Maintain a clean, clutter-free space, enough lighting, a comfortable chair, and distance from domestic distractions to ensure an effective work environment at home.

5.5. Boundaries and Communication

Creating a boundary between work and personal life in a remote setting is an ongoing challenge. Communication plays a pivotal role here:

Clear Expectations: Communicate your work hours clearly to your team. Don't hesitate to turn off notifications during non-working hours to maintain your personal time. Check-in and Check-outs: Start and end your day with a virtual meeting. It gives you a sense of entering and exiting the "work mode".

5.6. Staying Motivated

Remote work can sometimes feel monotonous, making motivation crucial:

Small Wins: Celebrate even minor accomplishments. It can be as simple as crossing off an item from your to-do list. These small wins can build into a sense of satisfaction and motivate you.
Rewards: Reward yourself for completing a challenging task. Personal incentives can be powerful motivators and can increase your productivity.

5.7. Managing virtual meetings

Virtual meetings could potentially be time-consuming and less productive if not managed efficiently:

Agenda & Time: Have a clear agenda for the meeting
shared in advance. Respect the schedule. Start and end
as decided.
Tools: Choose the right platform that suits your team's
needs. Understand the features and learn to use them
effectively.

5.8. Avoiding the Tyranny of Urgency

A common mistake in remote work is responding to every task like it's an emergency. The 'always-on' culture might make you believe you need to respond instantly. However, understanding the difference between urgent and important tasks can add hours to your day.

Remote work requires a different mindset and abilities than traditional office work, including advanced planning and effective communication. Regularly applying these strategies and finding what works best for you can make your journey in the digital world fulfilling and productive. Remember, the key to being productive is not about getting more done, but rather about focusing your time and energy on tasks that truly matter.

Chapter 6. Building and Sustaining Virtual Teams

In the DNA of every great organization, you'll find the golden thread of teamwork. No longer confined to shared physical spaces, teams are dynamically evolving within the fabric of the digital landscape. Building and sustaining virtual teams is both an opportunity and a challenge, ushering in a wealth of inventive strategies and methods.

6.1. Building Your Virtual Team

The inception stage of any team is of utmost importance. A successful virtual team starts with careful candidate selection and a meticulous hiring process.

Hiring the Right People: The first rule of thumb is hiring individuals with a knack for remote work. Some people thrive in an autonomous environment, displaying a self-starter attitude and high levels of motivation, while others need the structure of a physical office setting. Proficiency in digital tools, excellent communication skills, and sound time management should be some of the key criteria in your selection process.

Remote Onboarding and Training: Bringing a new hire onboard isn't simply about acquainting them with their roles and responsibilities. It's an opportunity to foster a sense of belonging, to instill in them the values of your organization, and to set them off on their journey with the right knowledge and resources. When done remotely, the process needs to be even more comprehensive and engaging. Consider deploying a combination of self-paced learning modules, live virtual orientations, interactive meet-and-greet sessions, and mentor-buddy programs.

Defining Roles and Expectations: Clear communication of roles, responsibilities, and expectations is even more crucial in a virtual environment. Make sure to provide detailed job descriptions, performance metrics, and project timelines. Include processes for regular check-ins and updates.

6.2. Fostering Collaboration and Communication

Once the team is set, the real work begins. In a virtual setting, the need for explicit and effective communication is magnified.

Virtual Communication Tools: Virtual teams rely heavily on technology for communication. Ranging from emails and instant messaging to video conferencing and collaborative documentation, mastering these tools is key to seamless interaction. Make sure the team is comfortable using these platforms and has access to training if necessary.

Regular Meetings: Despite geographical distance, virtual meetings serve to bridge the gap, facilitating real-time collaboration and dialogue. Regularly scheduled team meetings, one-on-ones, and brainstorming sessions help maintain team synergy.

Creating Spaces for Casual Interaction: Water-cooler chats and post-meeting discussions play a vital role in fostering team bonding and camaraderie. These informal exchanges, though harder to facilitate virtually, should not be overlooked. Consider setting up virtual lounges or dedicated meeting-free time for casual conversations.

6.3. Developing Trust and Accountability

Trust is the adhesive that binds a team together, more so in a digital setting. Building trust and ensuring accountability within your team will strengthen engagement, increase productivity and encourage positive work relationships.

Encouraging Open Communication: Fostering an environment where ideas and opinions can be freely expressed boosts mutual respect and trust. Include your team in decision-making processes and encourage them to voice their thoughts and feedback.

Providing Feedback and Recognition: Regular feedback and recognition foster a sense of accountability while also validating the efforts of the team. A blend of both public and private recognition can be instrumental in inspiring and motivating team members.

Leading by Example: As a manager, lead with integrity, transparency, and consistency to establish trust. Regularly communicate, show commitment to timelines and deliverables, and be responsive to your team's needs and concerns.

6.4. Adapting and Sustaining

Finally, remember that building a virtual team isn't a one-time endeavor - it requires continuous effort, adaptability, and resilience.

Keeping Up with Tech Trends: As digital landscapes evolve, so should your team's tech capabilities. Encourage the team to stay open to new tools and technologies and provide necessary training and resources.

Flexibility: Virtual teams embody flexibility – in working hours, environments, and resources. Know that the one-size-fits-all approach doesn't work here; allow for individual work styles while maintaining team harmony.

Sustained Learning and Development: Foster a culture of continuous learning and development. Regular training sessions can help keep the team's skills on point and relevant, encouraging professional growth and job satisfaction.

In conclusion, building and sustaining a virtual team is much like cultivating a garden; it requires time, care, and constant attention. However, with the right strategies, tools, and a shared vision, your virtual team can bloom into an indomitable force radiating productivity and positivity.

Chapter 7. Communication and Collaboration: The Virtual Edition

The switch from traditional office environments to remote set-ups illuminates the necessity for robust communication and collaboration. As the lifeblood of any business, it manifests in the form of project discussions, team huddles, brainstorming sessions, and more. However, when trading cubicles for computer screens, companies need to adapt and rebuild this critical framework.

7.1. Digital Communication: More Than Words

Effective communication in a remote setup extends well beyond simple emails, chats, and video conferences. Organizations must commit to fostering an environment of transparent, frequent, and hassle-free communication that brings teams together and nurtures a sense of belonging. But, not at the cost of clarity, conciseness, and precision.

Remember, good communication is always two-way. Ensure your messages are seen, understood, and responded to, with virtual platforms like Slack, Teams, or Basecamp. Leverage built-in features, such as "reads," "receipts," or "reactions," as acknowledgment tokens.

Moreover, periodic video calls or "virtual water coolers" can help psychologically and combat the distress of isolation. But, remember to respect "Do Not Disturb" statuses, time zones, and work-life boundaries. It's about getting the job done, not online presenteeism.

7.2. Understanding Collaboration Tools: Your New Co-workers

Collaboration tools are no less than colleagues in the virtual work world - capable of assigning tasks, monitoring progress, enabling brainstorming, and more. Tools like Asana, Trello, or ClickUp offer a digital snapshot of what's being done, by whom, and when. They paint a living mural of work progress while fostering accountability and #teamwork.

Consider the following while choosing your collaboration tools:

- The maturity and size of your team

- The complexity and domain of your work

- The need for real-time or asynchronous collaboration

- The necessity for integrations with other tools

- Your team's tech-savviness and willingness to learn new tools

- Security, confidentiality, and privacy requirements

7.3. Email Etiquettes: The Unseen Handbook

In the sea of virtual communication, emails, like ancient ships, have endured and proven their mettle. They remain relevant and robust for formal and asynchronous communication. But, wading through an overflowing inbox can be daunting. Hence, practice and propagate effective email habits:

1. Use precise subject lines.

2. Encapsulate the purpose in the email's opening lines.

3. Utilize effective formatting: bulleted or numbered lists, bold key

points, etc.

4. Avoid long emails. If it takes more than a minute to read, consider calling or scheduling a meeting.

5. Use CC and BCC judiciously. Don't flood inboxes.

6. Answer all questions. Address each point if multiple queries were raised.

7.4. Navigating Video Conferences: From Awkward to Awesome

Video conferencing is an excellent tool for face-to-face interactions in a remote setting. It promotes effective communication and adds a personal touch to the digital work environment. However, many people find these experiences awkward and stressful.

Here are a few tips to make your next video call smoother:

1. Check your tech before the meeting: camera, microphone, and internet connection.

2. Be on time.

3. Be present and avoid multi-tasking.

4. Follow defined agendas. Stick to the assigned slot.

5. Keep your background professional and distraction-free.

6. Dress appropriately.

Remember: The key to productive video conferences lies not just in the technology, but in how we utilize it.

7.5. Cultivating a Virtual Culture: The Invisible Bond

Culture is the binding force that provides context, fosters understanding, and promotes shared values. For remote teams, there's no communal lunchroom or break room for casual interactions. Hence, cultivating a virtual culture is vital.

Adopt virtual coffee breaks, online gaming sessions, or book clubs. Celebrate birthdays, work anniversaries, and other special events. Allow non-work conversations to cultivate connections. Encourage teams to share about their cultures, hobbies, or family.

Building an online community does not only improve camaraderie but also helps in understanding and respecting each other's work styles, eventually leading to better collaboration.

7.6. Asynchronous Communication: The Unsung Hero of Remote Work

Asynchronous communication, like emails, recorded video messages, or project updates on collaboration tools, allow teammates to consume and respond to information at their own pace. This becomes crucial in a globally distributed team where synchronizing with different time zones can be a challenge.

Encourage writing over talking. Documentation promotes clarity and serves as a reference point. Foster a mix of synchronous (for immediate decision-making) and asynchronous communication (for deep work).

So, step back from the clicking keys and let this sink in. The challenges of digital communication and collaboration are real but overcome them, and you are on a fast-track to an efficient, productive, and pleasant remote work experience. Remember, successful remote work is equal parts persistence, adaptability, and empathy. Happy remote working!

Chapter 8. The Challenges of Remote Work and How to Overcome Them

In the wake of the global pandemic, companies worldwide have been forced to reconsider their operational strategies. The sudden shift from bustling office spaces to the digital sphere has paved the way for a new work protocol. This transition, while beneficial for many, brings along with it its unique set of challenges.

8.1. Adapting to New Technology

The first hurdle in the path of remote working is adapting to new technologies. Whether it's mastering video conferencing tools, understanding project management software, or navigating shared documents, the technical aspect of remote work can be daunting. Employees must leap up the formidable learning curve while continuing to meet their professional obligations.

To overcome this barrier, invest time in training and support. Providing staff with easy-to-understand manuals, troubleshooting guides, or even organizing virtual training sessions can make it easier for them to adapt to new tools. It can be worth exploring user-friendly software equipped with detailed guides and responsive customer support. Learning should be seen as an ongoing process. Encourage team members to share their knowledge and tips on using these applications effectively.

8.2. Combatting Isolation

Working from home can quickly translate into feelings of isolation if not managed well. Gone are the water cooler chats and impromptu team lunches. The key is to make deliberate efforts to stay connected and foster a sense of camaraderie among the team.

Scheduled virtual coffee breaks are an excellent way to rekindle team spirit. Regular virtual team meetings are also crucial. Not just to keep everyone up to date, but to allow employees to see each other and maintain interpersonal relationships. For a more informal setting, consider creating chat groups for non-work discussions. In these challenging times, let the virtual window to your colleague's living room serve as a reminder of the human connections that stay steadfast despite physical distances.

8.3. Maintaining Productivity and Motivation

Without the regular office environment and work hours, maintaining productivity and motivation is another challenge. At home, distractions abound. Moreover, the boundary between work and personal life can blur, leading to work-life imbalance.

To tackle this, establishing a routine is essential. Create definite working hours and communicate this to colleagues to avoid interruptions. Build in short breaks to rest and recharge. An organized and dedicated workspace, free from distractions, can mimic the office environment and aid in focusing on work tasks.

Encouraging staff to set personal goals and rewarding their accomplishments can maintain morale. Managers should regularly check in with their team members, not only to discuss work-related matters, but also to understand how they are coping and if they need additional support.

8.4. Managing Communication

Without face-to-face interactions, communication can become an issue in remote work. Misinterpretations can occur, and messages might be read in a tone they weren't intended to be. Also, the lack of immediate feedback can trigger uncertainty.

To improve communication, establish clear and concise communication guidelines. Use video calls when discussing complex matters instead of relying solely on emails. This allows participants to pick up on non-verbal clues which otherwise could be lost. For important messages, consider verbal communication rather than written. Always make room for clarification and make it a point to ask if the message has been understood as intended.

8.5. Tracking Work Progress

Managers may find it hard to monitor team progress as they do in personal settings. This lack of visibility can lead to difficulties in ensuring deadlines are met with the same efficiency.

Implementing data-driven management allows managers to keep track of team productivity. Consider using project management tools that provide real-time updates on tasks underway or completed. Encourage staff to update their work progress regularly. Regular virtual meetings can facilitate discussions on work progress and the next steps.

In conclusion, while remote work does present challenges, it is undeniably the way forward. Therefore, addressing these challenges head-on and creating a supportive and inclusive work culture, despite the physical distances, will contribute significantly to adapting to remote working. Remember, irrespective of the hurdles, the goal remains the same – a motivated, satisfied, and high-performing team. By adopting and mastering the solutions suggested above, businesses can not only survive but thrive in the remote-working environment.

Chapter 9. Staying Healthy and Balanced: Self-care in Remote Work

Working remotely comes with many benefits, but it can also offer its fair share of challenges. This chapter focuses on the vital aspect of maintaining health and balance while navigating through the remote work world. This includes physical and mental well-being, ergonomics, and boundary-setting, among other areas.

9.1. Understanding the Importance of Health and Balance in Remote Work

Working from home can be a paradigm shift for many. In the hustle and bustle of completing tasks, meeting deadlines, and managing personal chores, it's easy to overlook self-care. In fact, surveys have shown that remote workers often struggle with unmanaged stress, poor diet, and lack of regular exercise. These factors can significantly affect productivity and job satisfaction, making it critical to maintain health and balance in a remote work setup.

With a remote work arrangement, you are in a unique position to tailor your work environment to promote your physical and mental well-being. The importance of this cannot be overstated. A healthy employee is not just more productive, but they are also more engaged and satisfied with their work.

9.2. Setting up an Ergonomic Workspace

An ergonomic workspace is designed with your comfort and productivity in mind. Sitting hunched over a laptop on your couch may seem convenient, but it can take a toll on your body over time. When setting up your workspace, consider the following guidelines:

- Desk and chair: Select a desk and chair that promote good posture. The top of your computer screen should be at or slightly below eye level so you're not straining your neck. Your chair should be at a height where your feet are flat on the floor, and your hips and knees are at a 90-degree angle.

- Keyboard and mouse: Buy a separate keyboard and mouse if you're using a laptop. They should be placed so that your elbows are close to your body and bent at a 90-degree angle.

- Breaks: Take periodic breaks to move around and avoid sitting or standing in one position for too long. Stand, stretch, or walk for a few minutes every hour. Use these breaks to rest your eyes as well.

Remember, the key to an ergonomic workspace is to ensure regular movement and comfortable posture.

9.3. Maintaining Your Mental Health

While the physical aspect of remote work is important, it is equally vital to take care of your mental well-being.

- Mindfulness: Practice mindfulness to manage stress and improve focus. This can involve a variety of techniques such as deep breathing, visualization, and meditation. Consider using apps that guide you through mindfulness exercises.

- Regular work hours: Set regular work hours and stick to them. When the workday ends, step away from your workspace to create a clear distinction between your work and personal life.

- Social interaction: Make time for social interaction to prevent feelings of isolation. This can involve virtual meet-ups with colleagues, calls with friends and family, or taking part in online forums and communities.

- Seek help: If you notice persistent low moods, anxiety, or other mental health concerns, seek professional advice. Many therapists and counselors offer virtual sessions.

9.4. Eating Well and Staying Active

Maintaining a balanced diet and regular exercise is crucial for your overall well-being.

- Diet: Plan your meals in advance to avoid unhealthy snacking. Include a variety of fruits, vegetables, lean proteins, and whole grains in your diet. Stay hydrated throughout the day.

- Fitness: Incorporate exercise into your daily routine. This could be a walk around the block, a home workout session, or following a virtual fitness class.

- Breaks: Use your breaks wisely. Go for a short walk, do some light stretching, or engage in a quick workout. This will help you stay fit and provide a much-needed break from work.

Remember, the key to staying healthy and balanced in remote work lies in maintaining a consistent routine, taking measures to ensure both physical and mental health, and maintaining boundaries between work and personal life. These steps should not be overlooked amidst work pressures and deadlines, as they directly contribute to your productivity, job satisfaction, and overall quality of life. The investment you make in your health and well-being is an investment in your professional success. Take the lead in this aspect, and you'll see a significant difference in your remote work experience.

Chapter 10. Leading from Afar: Remote Leadership Skills

In the era of remote work, leadership skills must evolve. No longer confined to a physical office, leaders are tasked with guiding their teams through a digital universe teeming with unique challenges. Notwithstanding, it also offers exceptional opportunities for those willing to adapt and thrive.

While research extols the myriad benefits of remote work - from increased productivity to improved work-life balance - it presents demanding tests of leadership acumen. Whether you're a seasoned manager or a fledgling team leader, the effectiveness of remote leadership will greatly determine the harmony, productivity, and morale of your team.

10.1. Understanding Remote Work Dynamics

Remote work hinges on communication, trust, and the judicious use of technology. First, a comprehensive understanding of the dynamics prevalent in remote work is vital in fostering a robust, productive team. Acknowledging these changes will allow you to steer your team through the choppy waters of transition, instilling a sense of confidence and camaraderie.

In a physical office, impromptu discussions, traditional meetings, and even casual water-cooler conversations contribute to team cohesion. Remote work environments remove these spontaneous interactions, necessitating extra effort to engage your team and preserve your corporate culture.

Decentralized workspaces can also lead to feelings of isolation among team members. A strong remote leader recognizes these challenges and uses the tools and strategies at their disposal to combat such feelings and foster a sense of community.

10.2. Leading with Empathy

Emotional intelligence, once a nice-to-have, is now an essential leadership competency. Empathy is of paramount importance in remote arrangements, where non-verbal cues are often lost in digital communication. Remote leaders need to 'listen' with an attentive ear, understanding the implied emotions and intent behind texts and emails.

Implementing wellbeing checks, regular catch-up calls, or other supportive measures can help employees deal with their unique challenges. By showing genuine concern for their team's mental wellbeing, leaders create an environment of mutual trust and understanding.

Encouraging open dialogue about struggles, as well as successes, can open avenues for team members to support each other.

10.3. Effective Communication

Clear and concise communication is the cornerstone of remote leadership. Proper communication ensures everyone is in sync and understands their roles, responsibilities, and deadlines.

Weekly meetings, daily catch-ups, and one-on-one sessions all form part of a comprehensive communication pattern that bridges the gap of remote work. Be sure to summarize key points of discussions and decisions. Documenting these reduces chances for misunderstandings and provides a written reference if memory fails.

Online tools like Slack, Google Meet, or Microsoft Teams provide platforms for real-time communication. Learning to use these tools efficiently is vital while leading from afar.

10.4. Trust & Autonomy

The ability to trust your team is pivotal. This trust must be twofold - trust in their ability to do their job and trust in their responsibility even when not closely supervised. Support autonomy, encourage decision making, and resist micromanagement.

Flexibility is a key benefit of remote work. Allow your team to capitalize on this perk. Open discussions about preferred work hours, deadlines, and productivity methods can lead to a more effective, satisfied team.

10.5. Continual Learning & Upskilling

As remote workforces continue to rise, so does the need to ensure your team's skills remain cutting-edge. Regular training sessions can be instrumental in this. Encourage continual learning, by offering opportunities for upskilling and growth. Not only does this keep your team valuable, it also shows investment in their career development.

Professional development opportunities, mentorship programs, e-learning modules, webinars, and workshops can all contribute to creating a team of life-long learners.

10.6. Building a Collaborative Culture

Collaboration in a remote setting involves more than sharing documents or working together on a project. It's about fostering a feeling of unity, even when physically apart.

Create virtual water coolers - spaces where your team can engage informally. Initiating trivia contests, virtual book clubs, or even video game competitions can act as the team bonding glue.

The leader plays a significant role in creating this. Be the first to share a weekend success story or a daily motivational quote. Leading through example will encourage your team to interact more freely and foster a sense of belonging.

The transition into successful remote leadership may not be an easy one. The challenges are stark, and the dynamics are vastly different. However, with empathy, effective communication, trust, a commitment to continual learning, and fostering collaboration, leaders can motivate and guide their teams successfully – irrespective of how far apart they may be. The brave new world of remote work awaits. Your leadership can make all the difference.

Chapter 11. The Future of Remote Work: Trends and Predictions

As the corporate world grapples with the ongoing pandemic, remote work is swiftly transitioning from being a mere luxury to a necessity. The future is becoming increasingly dynamic, thus giving rise to significant trends and predictions that are shaping the landscape of remote work globally.

11.1. Technological Innovations Ruling the Roost

A critical factor harnessing the power of remote working is technology. Newer solutions are incessantly being birthed, addressing challenges often associated with distant collaborations. With the continued optimization of broadband and 5G technology, remote work is set to become seamless.

One significant technological trend is the progressive use of Virtual Reality (VR) and Augmented Reality (AR) for meetings. Anticipate a future where you put on a VR headset at home to 'walk' around your office, engaging and collaborating with colleagues as though you were all together.

Artificial Intelligence (AI) is another game-changer, with potential applications in managing administrative work and simplifying tasks. From autonomous scheduling to drafting responses, AI will hold a significant part in the smooth running of remote operations.

Expect to see increased adoption of project management and team collaboration tools very soon. The future of remote work will rely heavily on these technologies to increase efficiency and productivity.

11.2. Embracing Remote Work as the New Normal

For many organizations, the transition to remote work might become permanent. Companies such as Twitter and Facebook have already announced their intention to allow employees to operate remotely indefinitely if they wish.

This evolution stems from an increasing recognition of the myriad benefits that remote work provides. These benefits range from saving on office space costs to achieving increased productivity, as well as promoting employees' work-life balance.

11.3. The Gig Economy Booming

The allure of flexibility that remote work offers is set to propel the gig economy to new heights. More individuals are projected to take up freelance opportunities, while companies will increasingly outsource tasks to external professionals over the internet. This shift not only reduces overall employment costs but also facilitates a quick and efficient execution of tasks.

11.4. A Greater Emphasis on Mental Health

A key consideration for the future of remote work is the increased focus on mental health. Remote work arrangements can lead to feelings of isolation and burnout, making proactive mental health strategies important. Companies may resort to scheduling regular check-ins and promoting 'technology off' periods to help maintain their employees' resilience and mental wellbeing.

11.5. Demand for New Skill Sets

The rise of remote work propels the demand for different skill sets several notches up. Besides technical skills, abilities like time management, effective digital communication, and self-motivation assume higher importance. Organizations will seek these skills actively, and professional development opportunities will also adapt to meet these demands.

11.6. Reimagining of Workspaces

The concept of a traditional workspace is all set to undergo a dramatic transformation. Expect a future where companies invest in ensuring ergonomic and dedicated workspaces at their employees' homes. This change could also stir a revolution in interior design trends.

As we navigate these uncharted territories, it's clear that the future of remote work is full of potential. Developments in technology and corporate policy changes will continue to change the landscape, paving the way for an improved and efficient work environment. Regardless of the challenges, one thing is certain: Remote work is here to stay. Embrace the evolution, and strive to become a part of these exciting progressions shaping our tomorrow.